Amelia The Young Witch

Paul Kuipa

Published by Paul Kuipa, 2022.

AMELIA THE YOUNG WITCH

First edition. January 24, 2022.

Copyright © 2022 Paul Kuipa.

ISBN: 979-8201532130

Written by Paul Kuipa.

Also by Paul Kuipa

Testimony Of The Resurrected
In Love With A Siren
The Walk Of Faith
Amelia The Young Witch

FORWARD

Amelia the young witch is a true based story of a young girl who suddenly initiated into witchcraft and voodoo. This story is going to shock you while some scenes will be exposing the secrets of the dark kingdom and its impact to the real world. As I know once read the materials of this book it will change your way of thinking, and even your belief way possible.

ENJOY

CHAPTER ONE

"Hey you daughter of Florence what kind of behaviour is that? You want me to vent out my anger on you so that my blood pressure will surge rapidly? Answer me! You child of a prostitute and a bastard Why you still staring at me so hard like you have seen a ghost? "Instead of keep doing your chores, is it a starring competition? Get out of my house now, and follow your mother. I think she's the right candidate to carry your entire burden.

Lucky, if you will still find her still alive. I think by now she has finished all the bars and clubs in many townships. That one she has the guts to stoop so low to the level of even dating dogs."

Every day of my life, I was being told such harsh words by my stepmother. Its true people say words hurt more than death. Definitely; I agree with them on this one. People fear death even more than pain. It's strange that they fear death. Life hurts a lot more than death. At the point of death, the pain is over." Death is that one thing everyone's afraid of, yet they will themselves to go on with life.

So although I wish I could swing my body off the top of a building, or walk into the depths of the ocean and stay beneath its waves, or shoot away the pain with the cool metal, I was hurt to the core by my stepmom's words.

Even if you accidentally drop a cup you'll be told what the beginning is, and what the end is.

Some people are in such utter darkness that they will burn you just to see a light. Try to take it personal.

Her lips: literally were made to spit uncomfortable and disgusting words. Venomous tongue you can't spot the difference between her and a snake.

There are people in life out there, which will make you feel uncomfortable whenever they are around. It's as if they were born to humiliate you, distract you, and get in the way of your success and happiness. I think that's the best way to describe her character. That's my stepmother I am talking about, her name was Stephanie. She was an evil second from the devil, when we talk about ranks of wickedness.

Sometimes I get beaten for no reason at all in front of her children. It was a way to humiliate and try to chase me away from her house.

It's not that I was an orphan no, Daddy was there staying with us at the very same house. My real biological father Instead of defending me, protecting me, or doing something nope, he will be starring, sitting on his big couch watching 14 inch black and white TV. Seemed to be enjoying seeing me in pain Always taking his queen's side and ends up blaming me for something I did not do, everything was my fault.

You never know how strong you are, until being strong is the only choice you have.

I grew up being called child of a prostitute, terrible names. Just because my mother was impregnated by a married man and denied the pregnancy after separation with daddy.

Father was having another relationship outside marriage which contributed to their downfall of their twenty one year relationship. Due to the pressure of what the future holds, raising me with the absence of my father. She dumped me at my father's house and went away a couple of days after my birth. I was born one year and nine months old. By this time daddy was staying with that wife, I mean stepmom. My auntie was the one who took care of me until I was 4 years old. She was a beautiful loving soul with a caring golden heart. No beauty shines brighter than that of a good heart. That's when I started understanding the word happiness.

Oh! There is light at the end of the tunnel right?

My sudden happiness quickly grinded to a halt, when her husband died, this drove me to land back in the hands of my stepmother. I'll call her Stephanie. I encountered all what is called struggle, pain, and torture. Being like an orphan whilst your parents are alive just imagines the pain and depression.

When I'm feeling triggered by the world and everyone it is behind fifty feet of glass. Loving bonds become inaccessible. In this mode I have to take great care not to damage bonds of love, the relationships and people who are everything to my heart and soul. For in time the glass disappears and my love returns. I wish I could stop the triggering, but if I feel unprotected or left to fend for myself it returns - it is survival mode, cold and indifferent. Yet even in these times I am cognisant of my morality. I still make good choices. I can still imagine what the better version of me would want me to do and then carry that out. I can't undo the trauma I've been through, but I can adapt and overcome it.

This disturbed my childhood. I wasn't like other children at all. With all these questions with no answer spinning in my head when depression sets in. So I am the product of prostitution? What does my mother think about me? I think dumping me she was shy of me, I was an embarrassment to her. So what I'm going to be in life? Even the poorest or blind people, they take care of their children. So why me I think I'm a real living curse to people. Even my own father doesn't see me as her daughter anymore. I've become a punching bag to his wife and relatives. What exactly wrong I've done to them to deserve this torture?

Bitterness grew inside me and my heart became weary and heavy.

I was raised without love and peace, not taught to show grace and forgive... They knew what they were doing. I suffered and they drank it like fine wine, becoming intoxicated on their own power. All I felt was bitterness and with each passing year it grew like a tumour, pushing on the side of me that was serene, enveloping me in toxic darkness.

That's what they call depression and anxiety. Just imagine suffering from depression in early childhood. It explained the whole situation. But you know what? God is watching over us all the time, he can get revenge. I can say karma. What goes around comes back around.

My father impregnated another woman, and Stephanie finds out. It was a disaster and created a lot of tension between them. All that peace and fairy tale love story Puff!!!

Was gone

Father decided to leave the house for a while. I was doing form- three (grade- eleven) by that time. All the pressure and anger Stephanie has, was offloading it all on me. I was the victim there.

One day she made it clear to me that I wasn't welcome anymore to stay at her house. The sooner I leave and follow my father the better it will be for both of us. Or else she was going to kill me. Threats: was my only fear. I tried to stay but due to too much pressure I moved out, and went to stay with my father's little brother. I stayed a couple of years until it was too much for him as well. I wasn't a troublesome child. One thing I notice in life, it is a great disadvantage when luck is not on your side.

He wasn't able to afford all the basic needs I need for my everyday life. By the way, he had a family to look after. So I was another burden on his shoulders. I begged him to leave me in the rural area. Grandmother will take care of me rather than going back to live with Stephanie. That's how I started staying with my grandmother.

You know common challenges to unleashing the potential of rural areas include low productivity; underinvestment in agriculture and non-farm rural employment; lack of adequate infrastructure; poor occupational safety and health and working conditions; and limited or no access to services, including financial services

I continued with school, and was going into grade eleven now. There were only three of us: myself, grandmother, and her granddaughter. Her mother died during delivery due to lack of help. In rural areas you know, hospitals are far. You can walk for days or long hours with no transport.

Also no one helped granny's daughter. By providing a cart to carry her to hospital they didn't want to help her because they were saying she was the daughter of a witch. There were rumours about grandma to be well-known as a feared witch, and was responsible for her children's suffering and struggles. To me with my situation, I wasn't caring at all about these talks. I told myself that the best thing is that I was happier here than I was before. Also was having a friend to play with. She was a little younger than me by two years. We started bonding, and became besties. I will call her Pamela, that's the granddaughter.

CHAPTER TWO

Pamela was a beautiful, charming, adorable, slim, and a light skinned girl. Having a weird attitude though, that you can barely understand Sometimes she will start talking to herself as if she was speaking to someone else. To the extent of laughing and clapping hands

That was spooky. Only people who are not okay upstairs do that. When you call her, that is when she will be disrupted, then stops what she was doing. And start giving you all the attention you need. Other times she would fold herself on a corner sitting quietly. And you can tell that this person is flooded with serious thoughts.

When you call her that's where she will come out from her adventure and take in a few deep breaths, with her hand pressing her heart feeling her heartbeat slowing down.

It kept happening for a long time. Even though I was starting to get used to it this time I am talking about summer. As you know, hot days in summer are a very bad experience. This particular day the temperature was very high, it seemed cruel, burning everything on its surface.

It was scorching and perspiring, exposing to it was much teasing. Trees and plants seemed to sulk in the sun. They kept quiet, motionless out of the wind. Birds and beasts obviously were all gasping for breath.

When we were walking from school, we met up with boys from our school going home. We started walking together; these guys were staying near our village. One of the boys was called Darren. He was good at proposing to girls and talked too much at school. But in class he sees nothing. Fake people have an image to maintain. Real people just don't care. That was his real self. Always having one style on his head, shaved bald.

You will be able to see those bright eyes and cheekbones. Perhaps you aren't supposed to say that such a macho man is pretty, but he is, he is.

He started talking words of love to Pamela. I saw that she already liked the dude. That was her weakness, when it comes to men. Darren was a quite handsome boy, no girl said no to him. I heard him talking to Pamela.

Darren: Pamela! You know what? You are the reason for my smile, the day I found you. Will you let me be the reason for your smile?

In you, my life becomes whole; with you my days become bright. In your hands I would love to lay, this night and for the rest of my life!

You deserve the world and all the good things it has to offer. If I fail to find that world for you, I promise to give you mine.

Are you a Google search engine? Because you've got everything I've been searching for in life.

She was blinded by Darren's sweet words. They started walking together behind us slowly, holding hands lovey dove, and you can smell the scent of love. I was left walking with two other guys. The journey wasn't boring at all because they were fun, cracking jokes. They made me laugh out loud the whole way. After a twenty minutes' walk, a loud scream was heard behind us to where Pamela and Darren launched.

"No, no, no, help please! This is hurting, something is beating me." Said Darren

We systematically marched to where the noise was the loudest.

It was Darren screaming, running around, and favouring his back, legs, and head. At first we thought he was joking. Maybe he was trying to scare us, as he was a funny guy. He liked to surprise people.

But our thoughts weren't right this time. We realised some fresh beating marks registering on his bald head. Indeed; something was beating him, especially on his bald head, that's where the marks were more noticeable.

Fear struck us all; Fear is wisdom in the face of danger." It's a good thing to be tuned in enough to feel fear and figure out why it's there and what to do about it; that's what bravery is. You have to be brave to feel that fear long enough to analyse it and keep your self-control. Because when we learn about it, it gives us a real chance to care better for others when they are scared, to be kind when others need help.

We have to help him out, at least try to take him out of his misery.

Whilst struggling to figure out what was happening to Darren, Pamela started screaming as well. Doing the same moves which Darren was doing, running south to west with the speed of light like a headless chicken. She ran towards our home followed by me. Darren had to take care of himself.

Sometimes it is foolish to stay; the courage for running away must be summoned for your survival

I caught her without reaching far. After stopping her, we resided under a long tree for a while whilst comforting Pamela. Her body was marked with red lines of blood, as you know a light skinned person. It was terrifying to watch. What were those invisible things that beat her? Tears were streaming rapidly only her poor cheeks. This incident stopped when we were about to reach home just after crossing the river. From nowhere, we met with grandmother. It seemed like she was lonely waiting for us.

Her eyes were red eyes, like a landmine ready to explode.

My grandmother was a quiet person but when upset, she will turn into a monster. Her lips were shivering, the gratitude expression was telling the whole story. Her angry eyes were telling me that her brain was in a different mode, that she was switching gears from empathy to cold emotional indifference. And she directs this mode in our direction.

"Amelia!! Is this time to come home? Who will water the garden? You and Pamela are now into boys so much huh? Answer me; with your age you have no shame, do you?" Said grandmother stammering, breathing heavily

I was confused and twisted indeed. I wanted to tell her what happened to Darren and Pamela then stopped with these questions.

What made this old woman so angry like this? The time she was talking about was our everyday time when we came back from school. Then proceed to the garden. She wouldn't mind or get angry, why is there so much rage today?

Whilst in the middle of my thoughts, she took a whip from a tree nearby, holding my hand and Pamela simultaneously. That day, we were beaten like bandits, without mercy I don't forget it, it always escalated in my mind. She even refused to eat that night. When the dawn came I was barely moving, because of the pain. Every muscle has seized up.

My body was struggling to recover, to repair the damage. Unable to move with any grace, my movements were jerky.

After this incident, I started having unanswered questions about my grandmother.

What always surprises me, granny wasn't working. No one sent her money, even her own children. But every day we will see different kinds of food: tinned beans, biscuits, soft drinks, everything the list goes on and on in our house. Where did all these come from?

That was the question. I remembered we will not use lambs at night but candles. Where were they coming from?

Not even a single day I was sent to the shops to buy candles or see Pamela going to the shops to buy candles or food. School fees were being paid in time without any further delays or even in advance. We never run out of food or anything in this house. Another thing, every Thursday, grandmother will eventually put twenty empty sack bags outside to dry up. A whirlwind will suddenly appear from nowhere, and carry those empty bags away from us until we are unable to see them. There was always a time during the night where I would hear baboons screaming outside of our house. That's when I started recalling everything

Who will Pamela be talking to? What was beating them?

CHAPTER THREE

That's when I kind of started believing those rumours about my grandmother, maybe they were absolutely true. She was scary sometimes, always performing unusual behaviours. Maybe if I ask Pamela, I will get some answers. I was discussing this laying down, planning my next move.

Another thought came. So you want to ask Pamela about your grandmother's witchcraft? What will you benefit from hearing it? Is there anything you are not getting here? Your school fees are being paid in time, not even a single day you were being returned home your school fees not paid. Different fancy clothes you are wearing, nice food you are eating including being treated nicely and fairly. So about the witchcraft rumours about the person who is putting food on your table, what will it benefit you? Let bygones be bygones. What is wrong with you Amelia? Which place is better if you have been told to choose one, here or at your stepmother's house? I kept battling with different kinds of thoughts coming from every corner of my ears until I fell asleep.

The moment I closed my eyes, I was trapped in this nightmare. I dreamt sleeping the way we always sleep. Grandma on the bed, Pamela and me sleeping on the floor. Whilst sleeping, suddenly a thundering knock was heard at the door which was very violent. Indeed left the whole house trembling.

It was very loud; it was knocked three times then stopped for a while and repeated again.

You know the reality of things manifesting in a dream, it will be more alive and sensitive. Even if you cry... you will wake up feeling it that indeed I was crying like never before.

So with the way the door was being knocked, caused me to tremble in fear. This fear was my challenge and my demon to slay, for it will come until I do, unannounced and gnarly. The only way out is to order this brain to function, to demand solutions instead of laying still. So though it feels as if my bones have no more strength and my muscles are all out of power, I still haven't the option to remain still, to be quiet enough to choose how to react.

This caused me to cover my head with blankets waiting for the next knock. When it does definitely, I will wake up Pamela.

It knocked again but this time only two times very fast, and Quickly, Pamela responded by waking up heading towards the door. These days were the days of the Moon where it was not at its brightest. A candle or a lamp was needed in order to see a person who's next to you.

When I heard her waking up, I whispered, "Pamela, Pamela! Did you hear what I just heard right now? Go and look for matches and the candle so we can wake up grandmother." Remember it was like a dream, and the moon was not completely full, not showing inside so I was not seeing clearly.

She didn't reply, kept on charging forward. First, I thought maybe she wanted to look for a candle or a match box at the table. But heard her footsteps going the opposite direction towards the door. I whispered again, Pamela did you find matches and candles? I heard her turning the handle of the door without responding to me "Pamela! I shouted throwing blankets away from me trying to stop her. I stood up trying to find where matches and candles were. As you know how difficult it will be, trying to find things in the dark, your hands will be touching everywhere like a blind person.

Another thought came to wake up grandmother but I insisted not to because she slept previously being angry. So waking up here was just waking up to another terrible storm. The time I found matches was the time Pamela was getting out of the house. I tried to be brave to try stopping her.

Being brave means being afraid, or at least it does for me. The two go hand in hand. First is the fear, then the determination not to be ruled by it. I will always choose to face fear, to conquer it, for how else are we to make true progress in life

There was no time to look for a candle, I just ran outside following Pamela, lighting the stick of matches, covering it with my hand so that the wind would not blow it off. The box of matches fell down, I kept lighting the only matchstick I was left with in front of me. So I can see where Pamela was.

It was so dark that I tried to open my eyes and failed before realising they were open. Most night skies were the darkest of greys, but this one was pure black. It was like someone shut off the stars and moon.

From a distance, I saw something disturbing, scary and horrific like a figure, holding Pamela's hand. It was like a baboon or gorilla in shape, standing upright like a human being.

I heard my heart tearing apart with fear. Legs started shivering by themselves, followed by Goosebumps which were rapidly forming at the same time.

I felt the sweat drenching my skin, the throbbing of my own eyes, and the thumping of my heart against my chest. My fingers were curled into a fist, nails digging into my palm. I couldn't hear my rapid breathing, but I felt the oxygen flooding in and out of my lungs. Hesitantly, my eyes look at the deadly creature before me, preying on the dark. Fear tortured my guts, churning my stomach in tense cramps. It engulfed my conscience, knocking all other thoughts aside. And overwhelmed my body, making it drastically exhausted.

You can't even run. What I only did was scream a loud scream once, "grandmother."

I remember being given a thunderous slap, with a sickening thud. I felt it cover my small beautiful face. What slapped me was something invisible and terrifying. It hit me so hard to the extent of losing consciousness.

CHAPTER FOUR

Falling down was the last thing I recall. To my genuine surprise, the sun was shining when I woke up. I could barely see it through the window. I tried to turn my head to the other side but wasn't able to do so. I felt the muscles of my neck having a lot of tension and in a lot of pain.

One of my eyes we're totally swollen, blocking my vision. It was like having two faces.

The swelling was beyond more general, and puffy as exactly to resemble that of a person suffering from advanced torture.

Even to speak I wasn't able to. "Amelia! Amelia! Are you hearing me?" It was my grandmother who was sitting next to me when she saw me trying to move. I answered with a small still voice but nothing was coming out. They just saw my lips moving. She helped me sit by myself leaning on the walls of the room. Mrs Mayo, grandmother's best friend was there, staring at me from a distance. She was residing at the other side of the mountain. They were all inside including Pamela talking and laughing.

I was still disturbed about the incident that happened earlier on, last night. I tried to fix the puzzle, but was still seeing some holes. *I was dreaming right so why waking up like this?* The left side of my face was blue, black. *Maybe it's just a trick of my mind. I am still dreaming right, let me try to wave my hand and see.* As I did so I realised yes I was back to reality not a nightmare anymore. I tried several times to stand up but was failing to do so. Even to cry, my voice was nowhere to be found. What I was able to do, was only blinking with my watery eye only left seeing.

There's no such dream like this. Sometimes we try to trick our thoughts and the reality which is being displayed in our own eyes.

This wasn't an imagination at all or being in the dream land. *So does this mean I'm now disabled with one eye, or becoming blind?*

Mrs Mayo prepared a cup full of water, leaves of weed in it. Aw disgusting:

She ordered me to drink it all, "drink my child; some of it don't swallow it. Rinse your mouth for seconds then you will spit it out. This will make you feel better; your muscles where it is affected will relax. The pain will instantly vanish away."

As I was hesitating, I was given this look to drink that medicine by granny or else. "Don't you know that time like this, when the moon is not completely full, no one is allowed to go out at night." she added laughing," you'll be attacked by the unknown of the night. Only that your ancestors are strong indeed my child, some people will eventually die at the spot" said Mrs Mayo. Pamela was giggling at what she was hearing though it wasn't funny at all. *They think that I'm a dumb person. I know what I saw, and what happened.* I said to myself staring at them but truly speaking I was afraid.

Another thought of running away from the house came but where to go? After following the instructions, I started feeling some changes, healing sounding like playing its factor. Grandmother was quiet, not saying any word or commenting.

Granny was a quiet person; you don't know what she is thinking in her own world. Quiet people always know more than they seem. Although very normal, their inner world is by default fronted mysterious and therefore assumed weird.

Never underestimate the social awareness and sense of reality in a quiet person; they are some of the most observant, absorbent persons of all.

After a while, she walked out Mrs Mayo for a distance leaving me with Pamela. She tried hard to tell me funny stories even to crack jokes but I wasn't in the mood of laughing. She was pretending nothing happened yesterday. I told myself not to ask her.

Sun was about to set on its horizon, and it's time for laughter and chit chat all around; less complaining about the weather goes on as people reflect on the activities they did on that day. In Rural areas, some were herding cattle, others were working in the gardens, and you know, different activities just to keep them busy for everyday life.

The day was melting into night. The sun showing off one last time; by dyeing the blue sky; with orange, pink, and hints purple the scanty clouds hovering above Earth like broken glass shattered into a hundred pieces.

We ate but I didn't sleep the whole night. Not that I wanted not to, only of l being afraid of being attacked again. What if history repeats itself?

I dreamt again, something was knocking at the door. I worked towards it to see what it was. My hands started trembling and my eyes wide opened as I reached my hand towards the door knob. Something was behind there and it was anything not good obvious. My body feels hot and sweat started trickling down my neck. I gripped it tightly and twisted it. With every move I make, I get more and more terrified. My breath quickens as I hear the creaking of the door. Suddenly everything was silent and behind the door was just darkness. Once I saw that there was nothing there, my tense body relaxed. And woke up thank God nothing happened.

I didn't go to school for two weeks, Pamela did. Days passed with no bizarre experience. Every night I was asking them not to switch the candles off. Someday, my grandmother decided to visit her rural area home. Where she was born and raised. There was a funeral there, one of her extended family members had passed away. "I'm going to leave both of you here alone. You are now a grown up girl, you will take care of yourselves. It's only for two weeks, so behave. If you are afraid of sleeping alone I will ask Mrs Mayo's daughter-in-law to come and sleep with you until I return." We both agreed to the brilliant idea. Since I've started staying with grandmother, it was my first time seeing her paying a visit elsewhere. Especially; to a place where she will need to board a bus. It caught us by surprise, how did she hear the news of the funeral?

She didn't have a single phone, even a person to talk to except Mrs Mayo. Soon as she left, it all happened accordingly, Mrs Mayo's daughter-in-law came to sleep with us. She was a young charming adorable woman with a five month year old baby boy. First night, her child cried uncontrollably almost the whole night. The child refused to be nursed by the mother. She tried various ways you know to make a baby stop crying but to no avail. To us strangers it was an annoying baby, but to her he was the light of her life, a miracle from God and a gift. He cries like always in pain for so many different reasons.

Carrying the child on her back, and even bathing him with salt with water to remove negative energy, if there is evil presence will flee. None of these tactics works, frankly it accelerates the situation. She asked us to wake up and pray with her. So that whatever is scaring the child will leave us alone. We prayed until we started hearing baboons fighting outside and crying. Followed by Pamela who started screaming loudly as well.

This surprise, when the unexpected became expected.

Engage people with what they expect; it is what they are able to discern and confirm their projections. It settles them into predictable patterns of response, occupying their minds while you wait for the extraordinary moment — that which they cannot anticipate.

We continue praying, chanting to God. Our prayers caused something unexpected to happen, unfolding the fold that night.

CHAPTER FIVE

My story is very long so I promise to try to make it short. She kept crying, outside terrible sounds of the unknown escalated. Pamela stood up, sweating. "Amelia! Stop what you are doing right now? Can't you see you're hurting grandmother? Stop it" she said, throwing hands in the air.

What caused her to be in such mode in a short time? Pamela I know is not a person who

Lived in anger, but this moment she turned almost into a cartoon character, was lost in that moment and the torment her brain was in. I'd see it first in her eyes, then a tension of her muscles, an inability to think clearly soon followed. The rational Pamela was offline and the primitive one who reverted to this habit was in.

It seemed as if something wanted to come out from her stomach, which caused us to stop abruptly, waiting eagerly to hear what she wanted to say. But words were not coming out. She vomited something like a caterpillar, a huge horn with a big redhead, and then something like a mango seed covered with hairy things. These things were scary indeed; you won't even look at them twice. Mrs Mayo's daughter-in-law was now possessed with the Holy Spirit. You can tell, started moving back and forth despite carrying a baby on her back. Singing religious songs. Even a non-believer can believe right away, and suddenly to tap into the heavenly network.

To me, literally I was at my weakest point due to fear and shock which rocked me...

The paralysing fear spread through my body like icy, liquid metal. I will call her Julia or Ronald's mother. Minutes passed and Julia took the baby and laid him on the bed. Since my childhood, I have never attended a prophetic or spiritual church. I was a Catholic. So what Julia was doing was all new to me. Especially praying in tongues, was the strangest part. A person suddenly speaks a foreign language you can barely understand. Holding Pamela's head twist and turning it.

When I tried to stop her from hurting Pamela, she hit me with a header. I only saw stars then went down to the ground.

Within going far, stacking with this incident. A strong unusual sound was heard. It was very loud. It sounded like broken glasses being dropped three times on to the ground. In other ways it was like something, perhaps someone was trying to escape through that window. That day it was like a horror movie. I witnessed it with my own eyes.

Julia kept herself busy that night. Circled around the whole room several times, doing her things. Then suddenly fell down, like a person who lost consciousness. Three minutes later, she woke up and sat on the bed perfectly fine like nothing had happened. "Girls, if you know how to seek the presence of God, I think you should start right now, because there's an evil activity here, real witchcraft. What I am seeing is huge and stronger than me spiritually... Find God or someone to help you.

This kind of witchcraft I had never seen my entire life. I urge you my younger sisters to please start to pray violently because this kind of witchcraft is too much. I was born in a prophetic church then I left when I was married. My husband came and left me here to my mother-in-law, Mrs Mayo. You know what; she doesn't want anything to do with churches. She hated it to death, only about the ancestral stuff that's only she believes in.

Beliefs and things are only real if you believe in them, insanity can be in sanity if you do it right and keep all your intellect intact. In truth, it is the secret key to virtually infinite genius creativity. It comes at a cost though. Once you open that door you are in it for this spin of the mortal die and then you are eternally recruited for the team you served during your life.

Imagine how hard it is to have no time to pray. Sometimes, I would sneak out to the nearby mountains to pray alone but I'm telling you this witchcraft is terrifying and strong. Let's put it this way; every time I come here, we will pray so we can overcome this"

Pamela, how are you feeling right now? Pamela was lying exhausted on the floor. Julia took salt, mixed it with water, prayed for it then sprinkled the whole house and what Pamela had vomited. That night we didn't sleep the whole night talking about life and our past. Julia was talking about her experience through her prophetic journey.

When dawn sets, outside our house we had Mrs Mayo's voice for a distance by approaching our house. Matter of seconds she arrived yelling loudly knocking the door. "Why are you taking so long to just open a single door, open now?" she said, shaking the door handle violently which caused her daughter in law to step up quickly to her aid.

She was welcomed by a surprised slap. On the face right between the eyes, and stunned for a second. Sure the slap stings, but knowing you aren't in control of yourself is the greater cause for concern.

THIS OLD WOMAN WAS very angry indeed but what caused her to be in such anger mode? No one knows, especially in those early hours. "Why don't you have manners Julia? What are you doing in other people's houses instead of sleeping? You were making noises Disturbing things. Tell me! Are you a relative here to disturb things in this house?

Julia didn't respond, she just carried her baby on her back then started going followed by Pamela and myself. Before our feet touched the ground. Shocked by this incident, the whole yard was filled with black deadly scorpions scattered everywhere.

CHAPTER SIX

BLACK SCORPIONS WERE all over the yard. Julia screamed and ran back inside the house. There was no way to step on it. Mrs Mayo only shook her head, shouting loudly, "What my eyes are seeing? Holly Gracious, my ancestors, my dad who is resting in the grave. Come and witness these mysterious phenomena, which have been brought here by this stranger.

Who was called the stranger? Her daughter in-law.

As for us, we gathered ourselves around the corner. Yeah fear of cause. After staring at us for such a long time, she started doing incantations. Took out stuff from her bra which had a traditional cigarette on it. Started smoking, some she sprinkled it on the ground where scorpions scattered.

You know shock brings quietness within, a moment to feel the emotions changing gears and girder to the soul for what we were witnessing.

Where we were just looking at her in dismay, doing what she was doing. Even calling other people for help wasn't necessary because of the spacing of the houses in rural areas.

Though she scolded us, we were very worried, and felt pity for her daughter-in-law. She was the one being targeted the most and told not to respond back. We haven't been given time to explain ourselves to ask what wrong we have done.

She kept yelling and yelling for about an hour. That when we started witnessing the scorpions lining up heading up to where the chicken House was launched. Followed by loud screams of chicken seeming to be attacked.

Suddenly a breakout silence followed. We rushed to open it to save our chicken, but it was too late. All of them were dead, but the scorpions were no longer there. That was our last to see the black scorpions.

"Julia, let's go, you will see me at home. Amelia! Once your grandmother is back, the first thing to do is tell her to come to my house right away.

After they left, we were left alone again.

Time passed slowly. I stayed hidden with my head in the blankets feeling every beat of my heart pounding on the warm bed I was laying upon. The only one sound to be heard; was the sound of my own pulse throbbing in my ears. With the serenity of silence surrendered outside.

What if what happened repeats again? What would we do? I thought of running but where to go? I tried to be brave but my mind was telling me to go. I packed my clothes and told Pamela that I was going. She was going to take care of the house. What I value most was my life most. As I was dressing, she tried harder to stop me. "No, no you can't leave me alone here. I don't want to die here. I'm going with you. I tried to stop her but she refused until I agreed to go along with her. We took off straight to the bus station.

The distance was about only a kilometre walk away from our house. It wasn't a big station though. You could only find small cars to pick you up at the real station. When your brain is confused and twisted you will not think properly. We started thinking that, when we arrive at the station what we will say we are going? If we do well, who will receive us? We don't even have a single cent with us. Where exactly are we heading? I asked Pamela if she has a friend or somewhere she knows to go for a couple of days whilst figuring out a proper place for us to go.

Even relatives of his father but she said she doesn't know her father, as well as no relatives. The only relative she knew was grandmother. Her mother died during delivering her. Grandmother was the only one to raise her since she was born. We were seated on a huge rock trying to figure out what was our next move. She brought up the idea of us going to my father's house. That was a horrible idea because it was only I who knew my story and my pain. So going there will rewound my healed wounds. It was better to go back home and try to face our fears.

As we started walking back home, Pamela stopped abruptly and held my hand.

"Why did we stop?" I asked.

"Sister you know what; it's the same thing to run or to go back. Sam and Simon and others will follow us wherever we go"

Me: Who is Simon and who is Sam?

Pamela: These are my husband's. Promise me if I tell you this secret you will not tell anyone else.

"I promise" I quickly answered eagerly to hear next. "Just tell me, I promise across my heart and hope to die. It will stay between you, me and God." But my expression was changed showing shock was registering on my face.

Pamela: Let's go and sit on that side under this tree, so that I can tell you everything in detail. She narrated her horrifying story, I mean everything. Pamela: Grandmother has invisible things that can't be seen by naked eye. I mean your eyes, the eyes of the flesh. Only gifted people with their spiritual eyes opened. Sangomas, Wizards or prophets.

When I was young, grandmother had two big kids, goblins (spirits of dead people) which were only coming at night. She had to reserve the meat for them to eat. That was their only food. When it comes to sleeping time, she removes all my clothes and asks me to always sleep like that, naked. She forbids sleeping and being dressed because it will attract evil spirits. Then I brought these weird kids inside my blankets so that I can sleep with them. She said they were my friends; I should sleep with them and keep them warm. First days I was afraid and refused until I was getting used to them. Every time I get inside the blankets, they will follow. They ended up licking my fingers and my breasts until getting intimacy with them. I was not the only one sleeping with them, grandmother too.

Grandmother killed many men including Sam, Simon and Tobias. People she killed will turn him into a baboon or a cat or a goblin. When a person dies you will bury an empty coffin. Witches steal the body from the mortuary or once a person dies. They will project an image of the dead person and people will think that it is their loved one. But the real person is gone. Even during body viewing you will see that fake image laying in a coffin. Only people with spiritual eyes open can see the truth. They end up demanding too much a wife.

So that's where I come in place, being an everyday wife. They will come every night to sleep with me; I'm a married woman as you see. Amelia; so running away can't be necessary anymore. They all follow me around, even my young stepmother, Susan and Ruth, they all have husbands. Grandmother has them; they are both married to these spirits. They have roles of being sent by grandmother to steal money, food and different items from various people in the communities and shops. Those are the things you always see in the house.

CHAPTER SEVEN

ALL THESE WOMEN SHE was mentioning about none of them have ever got married or even stayed with a man in their entire lives. At first I didn't believe her, but the more she got deeper caused me to sit uncontrollably. Fear about what I was hearing. My hair was all pointing upwards followed by Goosebumps which were showing its presence on every part of my skin.

Me: Can't you stop, I am getting scared now of your story. Please say it's not true.

Ha.ha.ha. you think it is a joke? You think I am cooking it right? What you are seeing with your physical eyes is not the real world. Real stuff is happening unseen and it's the reality. What I can say Amelia, the physical world is all fake. As you see, grandmother has lots of secrets. She has three secret clay pots three. One is for blood; other is for short boys and lastly is with terrifying creatures of different types that can all patrol at night.

The one for blood is the scariest one. When you are closer to it. You will hear it producing a terrible unfamiliar sound like a running jet engine. Mostly; when it sounds like that, it's a sign that it is running out of blood, and requires a quick top up. If granny took time to bring another blood in time, she would start oozing out blood like a woman on her periods. That blood will automatically be collected by the short boys.

They are the ones who suck your blood by oozing blood and through sucking your breast. Then fill the clay pot of blood.

She said to the girl without hesitation or being afraid. It showed to her it seems normal but to a person like me I was unable to accept that this stuff exists. I was at a loss for words because I wasn't not sure how a soul as pure as hers has experienced and survived these paranormal activities and evilness of this world. She wasn't only soft hearted, but tough enough to stay that way. That takes a kind of bravery that I was still processing, hence the silence.

Pamela: Tobias is the one who really loves me and is jealous a lot. He doesn't want to share me with other boys. That day coming from school, he was the one who was beating us. Now he is upset that you broke granny's clay pot of blood with what you were doing with Julia. Your powers caused many bad things to happen and it's now a disaster.

She told me a lot of strange stuff. Some of it I will not explain because I will take time. Honestly speaking; I started to be afraid of her. I think I will run away from her but where should I go?

These are times which fry the brain. It's no excuse. I know my life was a mess. I am just a girl trying to live here. Then a trigger was flicked, my emotions turned - cold, fearful.

I started thinking about my mother. If she didn't dump me, I wouldn't be facing these situations.

Time was moving and the sun was now sitting on the horizon.

Dusk came sooner than expected, the last of the sun's rays cosseted behind soft grey clouds. The forest took on the look of an old photograph, every familiar thing turned into a shade of grey. Slowly the view faded to blackness and the night began.

Just imagine being confused, hungry, dirty and tired. Since yesterday we didn't sleep, we remained seated until dawn not knowing what to do. In my mind, I was cross about not going back anymore. Darkness started setting in, and we had to act very fast. With a rush decision, we decided to go to our neighbour's house who is staying next to us. Even our homes were spaced; that was our only plan and only option. I will name her Mother Ruth. When she saw us approaching, she ran to stop us at the door.

She left what she was doing to me," what do you want here? She asked, touching both sides of the door, blocking our way in. I tried explaining to her that; we were only seeking a place to sleep for one night only.

Our grandmother left us so we are scared of sleeping alone. People will take advantage of us and do whatever may deem necessary to harm us. Instead of helping us she started yelling at us. She ran to her bedroom quickly and came with a small bottle filled with salt water. Sprinkled at us on our faces yelling and scolding. Her husband tried and failed to stop her. She was like a possessed woman.

Mama Ruth: Now your grandmother has sent you here to finish me physically. She's using her witchcraft for her own evil purposes and you are all initiated. Who doesn't know that? The whole village knows about you. She tried sending the goblins to kill me three times but failed. And now it's you. Did you know she even sent a baboon as well physically to attack me because of beans and cooking oil I have received from the donors? She became jealous of why I had received them and he hasn't.

She was pushing us away bit by bit further away from her house. Her whole family rushed outside to witness the free drama, of us being humiliated to the core.

"Go and tell your grandmother that I came from the family of strong ancestors. Nothing will happen to me. You will do nothing to me seriously; trust me on this one "I started crying. You know, imagine being embarrassed in front of people like that. We had to move from her house to avoid being humiliated furthermore. With tears in our poor cheeks, we started returning home. It was a cold night. This type of coldness reaches into my bones, as if my heart were a door left wide open to the icy wind, slamming only to open again.

The only thing to do was to keep moving, keep heading towards home and the steady warmth of the hearth. The sky was a rolling blankets of cloud the colour of wet ash, and the ground its dank reflection. Each step becomes a prayer for home as we walk, seeing the light from the doorway in our flickering daydreams, letting it become, as finally we were approaching.

Pamela cooked, but I refused to eat that night. I didn't sleep the whole night thinking of two things, the words of Mama Ruth and being afraid. Maybe something will come to attack us like what happened the previous night. What if history repeats again?

I slept in the kitchen instead, where there was fire and with the candle burning the whole night.

When dawn set, when Cocks started crawling, grandmother had already arrived. I felt my gut twisting. What will I say? Because of fear I didn't even greet her. I ran outside to the toilet at a nearby Bush, my stomach was rumbling, but it was almost too late. I nearly pooped myself. I took almost two hours outside, even that morning wind, it wasn't a factor anymore. Pamela was the one who followed me. What are you still doing, from that time until now? "Grandmother needs you right now. You should come and wash her clothes and yours. But she is gone already see her best friend Mrs Mayo"

Was she looking angry? How was she looking? I asked you politely" I said.

Pamela: No she was not, only her ear is hurting her so much.

We went back home but my legs were still shaking. I washed our clothes. My mind was still worried about what would happen next. She came back after a couple of hours, both with Miss Mayo. I saw that she was wearing a fake smile and pretended as if nothing had happened.

Miss Mayo: Your granddaughters are very naughty very naughty. They were playing with my daughter-in-law Julia, to the extent of breaking things including that window. That one and I was very angry, I nearly beat them all. Granny was quite since but seemed to be in severe pain.

I knew my grandmother so well if something bothered her she will keep quite like a ticking time bomb waiting to explode.

She made herself home remedies of muthi (traditional medicines and drank it, trying to heal herself. Then gave me that left remedy in a cup to put it in a safe place. She wanted to rest a little bit.

Within minutes after she went inside the bedroom to sleep, she called me to bring the medicine. I looked inside the cup where water mixed with leaves and oil. It was very smelly.

She asked me to drop some droplets in her ear. Which I did and covered it with a piece of cotton. The whole night she was seated treating her ear repeatedly.

This really did disturbed her sleeping cycle. Nearly dawn when she woke me up to nurse her ear. I saw a small millipede making its way inside that ear. This caught me off guard, instantly I dropped the cup, "grandmother look at that millipede it's getting inside your ear"

CHAPTER EIGHT

THE CUP FELL FAR, AWAY from my hand at a distance like a stone thrown, spitting the medicine. I knew that I was in trouble and hid myself in a corner. As I was telling her about that thing inside her painful ear, instead of taking action quickly or trying to pluck it out, no. She just gave me a withering stare, which was terrifying.

"Amelia, you are now getting into my nerves, stop pissing me off in my own house. You and your little ugly eyes, you think you see everything. All what you have done with Julia in my house, Mrs Mayo told me everything. I didn't take you to disturb my peace and my things" Amelia who you think you are" She said while taking her tommy shoe which was hidden at the side of the bed. Threw it right on target, hitting the corner of my eye It hurt, I wanted to cry but hold myself. I was avoiding her to beat me.

"Yaa! Good, those eyes which see too much. Where is the other shoe so I can blind the other one" She was saying it while putting on those shoes and left the house immediately. It was obvious she was going to see her best friend to remove stress.

Elders believe that when you are angry go outside to freshen yourself so you can calm down. Many unusual strange things happened at this very house, so many strange things. I mean bizarre, but I'll try to make my story short. I started experiencing weird things when sleeping,

31

nightmares but forgets when I wake up. Sometimes I can wake up feeling that it was happening real.

Couple of days ago my vaginal area started itching severely. I will scratch and scratch until spots of tiny blood come out. Followed with a burning sensation. Pamela recognised it and told grandmother that I was sleeping with boys around. That's what she thought but which boys? One day when Mrs Mayo was around talking and laughing with her friend. Suddenly that story came up of me starting dating.

Mrs Mayo: Lay down so I can have a look at you down there. I want to know if these rumours are true, sleep on

Your back. She opened my legs wide open, put her two fingers inside like she was taking out something. I felt a small pain, and tried to sit so that I'll have a look at what she was doing. She pushed me back to sleep. Surprisingly; I heard a small sound like a baby rat squeaking three times after she finished. It felt like she was inserting something else I don't know.

"Stand up, my child, you are still a virgin. It's that you are not washing your underwear nicely. Young girls must be taught how to wash their undies properly. Only that you are coming small worms, which is normal and caused by that infection. That's why it's itchy and reddish. It's not that they are eating you now. Stand up I'm done with you by tomorrow you will be ok my darling, don't worry"

I saw a small cloth filled with my blood which she was using. When I wanted to wear my panties, only to notice that I wasn't able to. My pubic area had herbs like jelly, very slippery and disgusting smelling too. Meaning that, the medicine will work to kill the small worms.

Tomorrow morning, I saw blood spots on my paint. What periods? My period passed a week ago. Am I going again? I didn't know that this old woman was already planning for me and my virginity. I realised later that she was putting witchcraft marks on my pubic region to initiate me. And surely all the itching and swelling was gone. I spent almost the other two weeks being fine.

One fine morning the early bird went tweet-tweet; just as the first rays of sunlight creped over the hills. The air was light, crisp and refreshing; with hidden traces of ocean breeze. The early risers were grateful for the bright day. Within minutes the air became heavy and thick as the sun fully revealed itself. It hung in the morning sky like a brand new golden coin glowing with radiance.

I woke up feeling tired and weak like a person who was sick for a long time. And caused me not to go-to school that day. Grandmother was sitting in the kitchen preparing seeds for the fields. I helped her a little bit, then left her and went to the bedroom to sleep for a moment. It was where favourable temperatures were. I laid on my bed relaxing then instantly; started feeling like a person who was experiencing sleep paralysis. Let me try to break it to you, about sleep paralysis and what other religions and scientists have to say about it.

Sleep paralysis is usually caused by demons, witches or spirits who will visits you at night. Some demons will end up sleeping with you... sometimes you will call for help but you will find out that you have lost your voice.

According to scientists, it's different. You're waking up or falling asleep, and suddenly you're unable to move. Your body becomes paralyzed as if an unseen weight is upon you.

You may be unable to move your arms or legs, body and head. You can breathe and think, but you may be unable to speak.

Sleep paralysis occurs when the line between sleep and wakefulness is blurred. Normally your brain paralyses many of your muscles during the stage of rapid eye movement sleep – or REM sleep. This paralysis is called "atonia."

You may experience sleep paralysis if atonia lingers as you wake up from REM sleep; it also may occur if you transition quickly from wakefulness into REM sleep. Sleep paralysis may occur together with hallucinations. You may imagine that you see or hear something; you even may think that someone else or something is in the room with you.

Sleep paralysis can be a very scary thing. In it, you know you're asleep, you try to wake up, but you can't. It's often accompanied by an irrational feeling of utter terror, and sometimes images of figures in black cloaks. But one word to describe it, it's all witchcraft.

But I was aware of my surroundings. Moments later I saw a man dressed in a blue t-shirt and grey trousers coming inside the room to where I was. As I was attacked by sleep paralysis. I was unable to move or to stand or to run away.

He came to where I was not talking and started undressing me and took off my pants and threw my dress away from us. I tried to scream but words were not coming out. He didn't remove his clothes and lay on top of me then started acting like a person who was sleeping with me. I was trying to move but my body froze; only my eyes were able to move. He started doing his job, I felt it the sexual pleasure for the first time in my life. I felt his sexual organ getting inside me I don't know how because he was wearing his clothes. A thought clicks instantly that it was Mrs Mayo's doings and those initiation marks causing all these things.

I was feeling all the pleasure and I was enjoying the serious talk. I never sleep with a man. That was my first time experiencing this for the first time. After he finished sleeping with me, I saw him leaving through the door leaving me. Another surprise was that the door was closed but he went through it. It seemed like the doors and walls were transparent to him. I felt very exhausted more which caused me to fall asleep. When I woke up Mrs Mayo was outside racing a chicken.

"Amelia come, help me to catch this stubborn chicken. I am failing to catch it." She said falling down when a chicken was hiding between her legs, which caused her to fall on her face to the ground. You can't laugh at adults if they fall, we were always forbidden. They said it will bring bad luck. This incident of this man coming to sleep with me wearing the same clothes, repeats again for the second time. Whenever I am alone he can come through the closed day and wasn't talking. Just sleep with me and go. The third time when it happens. This man when he was in the middle of sleeping with me, he started changing into a baboon. I was scared and tried to fight him but was too paralyzed remember. He didn't stop f****** me. This is the time or a situation which caused a person to lose consciousness but I didn't, I don't know why.

CHAPTER NINE

SOME OF YOU FOUND FAVOUR and Grace in life by never encountering such problems. I'm not asking you to judge me or not to people like me because it's not by choice but by situation. What I am telling you it's not fairy tales or fake stories but real life encountering stories. This is really happening in many people's lives out there today. I remained laying down because I was exhausted every time. With my private part in pain. When this human- baboon was gone, I looked down to check because it felt something flowing on my thighs.

It was watery sperm running down my legs. When it reaches down it gathers together and forms something like rotten milk instantly. It was scary and disturbing at the same time. I ran out of the room to my grandmother.

"Look grandmother" I said pointing my finger down to show her. Instead of getting shocked by these phenomena, she stood up and scolded me.

Granny: What are you crying at? Whom do you want to hear you screaming?

She took a whip that was the time Pamela was coming inside from school. I ran and hid behind her. Even though she tried, her whip stick was still reaching my legs. She dragged me and took me to the bedroom then locked the door. That's where I was beaten very hard. After she started feeling guilty and started sobbing. You know the crying of an old woman with old tears streaming down her cheeks. I wanted to ask grandmother what wrong I've done to you.

Grandmother: What wrong have I done to you, my child? I took care and raise you since you were young, when you were dumped by your father. I am now understanding that I have made a huge mistake. Maybe I have what I wronged you somewhere, somehow. I am paying school fees for you, everything you need I am giving you. Is there anything you're not getting here?

Sorrowful tears showed streaming on her cheeks again.

What is wrong with this woman? I asked myself.

"Maybe it will be a good idea if you pack your bags and leave my house. And go to those who will give you everything you want in life because I'm failing you.

I was now out of words and afraid of the way she was behaving. I didn't do anything wrong to her. I just showed her what was on my thighs and received a beating for that. She took my bags and put my clothes including uniforms and took some money and gave it to me. "Take it and go" She threw them outside then rushed inside to continue what she was doing.

Another thought came saying that it was the best way if I left the house for good. But the other one was resisting saying where would you go. Plus it was time I should write my final exams. I remained standing not knowing what to do outside. Grandmother was pretending as if she was not seeing me, I was seeing her staring at me with the corner of her eye. I don't know how I reached where she was. I found myself on my knees holding her hand, begging for forgiveness. She kept pretending she was not hearing what I was saying at all. I didn't move a muscle but kept on begging and begging. After a while, that's when I was told to bath and eat.

Granddaughter: I think we should start working together for your own good. So that I can continue raising you and taking care of you. But if you don't agree you are free to go my child the door is open. You can be whoever you want, wherever you want to go.

She was calm and normal again, "I can't explain to you what is happening here. It's better for you not to know much for now. How many years being here and I never force you a single day to stay. You do whatever you want. So if you don't want to do what your grandmother wants you to do it will not be a good thing. Like Pamela is still alive and kicking today because she agreed to do what I was asking her to do. She was supposed to be in the graveyard by now with the ancestors. Pamela come and fetch me that bag of food"

Pamela ran and came with the bag with small charms including ginger and gave me to chew. After that I should spit it and swallow its soup which is squeezed. I did everything as I was instructed as a person who was out of options and afraid of being kicked out. She said tomorrow was supposed to go with me somewhere. Tomorrow arrived, while it was still dark we were already on our journey. I asked Pamela to accompany us but my grandmother refused wholeheartedly. I was the only one to go with her. We walked and walked through dark scary forests. It was a long journey though.

I think it was a whole day's journey. I think it was around four when we reached a big cave. Behind it was a strange river which was known to reside a mermaid. So no one wanted to reach that side. Because that place carried a history of people getting vanished in that river and the cave. As we arrived at another second cave, you were not able to see what was inside it. Was totally dark, you couldn't see if it kept extending or what. I was instructed to remove my shoes and clothes which I did.

She threw a stone inside the cave. I had an echo sounding of the stone rolling, falling inside and kept on going. It seemed as if someone caught it and kept throwing it further paul further. She takes the second one and throws it and does the same.

The third one she gave me meant it was my turn to throw it. I was supposed to throw it with my left hand. I did but I didn't hear any sound as if someone was catching my stone.

When I was still wandering, that's when I saw a huge, very big monstrous snake. I had never seen a snake like that before, it was scary indeed the way it was coming out of the cave. My legs were shivering and I was failing to stand or to run or even to breathe. The monstrous creature was approaching where I was with the speed of light.

Honestly speaking; my mind was in total shock, I went blank for a moment. My heart was beating in my ear and I was breathing heavily.

Seeing that monstrous beast that hugs the ground, soulless, dark, and menacing.

"Be strong, my child, to make this work. If you make any noise or any movement you are dead. Shut your mouth" It came and stood right in front of me looking exactly in my eyes. It puts its tail down then stands upright the same size as a man.

I didn't move a second and I felt it smelling the air like she was smelling my fear. Then returned to where it was coming from. Grandmother started following it going inside. She didn't take time and came out holding sorghum mealie-meal and rapoko.

To me I was still on my knees, unable to move or to stand. She sprinkled water on my face and applied that mealie meal she was having on my back and helped me to stand up. She went with me inside the cave and brought me out three consecutive times. Chanting with a foreign language. I didn't think I would see this level of witchcraft like this again. Beloved ones, this is how I was initiated into witchcraft, the kingdom of darkness.

CHAPTER TEN

SHE GAVE ME WATER TO drink so that I will recover strength.

Granny: What you have seen my child, proves that you are strong enough. Because if you were not, you were supposed to die instantly at the spot after looking at that snake. So what you saw should remain in your eyes, not in people's ears do you understand? Because that will be your last time. The snake you saw is not a snake but it's the spirit of our ancestors. That's where we get powers to protect ourselves. As well you and Pamela, nothing will harm you.

The world you see is not what it is. Bad things happen especially to good people. Look closely, I want you to always remember the way so that you will not get lost whenever you come with Pamela when I'll send you. That time will come when you'll be coming alone here.

I put on my clothes, started our journey back home. What surprised me, when I came out of the cave, I wasn't myself. I felt like something took over my body. First I wasn't scared anymore and was feeling brave. From that day on, I started seeing strange things and invisible stuff. In the house, outside or even if walking. Things walking with people, spirits of ghosts, and even witches. As I was initiated I was no longer afraid of these experiences.

It was true; grandmother was having goblins or short boys, magical creatures, four of them.

I saw them with my own eyes. Three of them were white, very short. Their size was half a metre I guess. The fourth one was a black man. All boys, no females. I started being taught things of witchcraft and was shown different places where Granny thinks her things are hidden and receive her witchcraft stuff and powers.

Including a spiritual lightning. People don't understand when I say lightning; Yes the real lightning we always see lighting the whole dark sky, travelling from north to south with a speed of sound. That one we see always when there is a storm. Yeah, some it's Mother Nature but some it's for sorcerers, witch and wizards controlling them. It will be in different various forms before being sent into the sky or to the victims.

My grandmother's lighting was in the form of a tree bark. A string you strip from the tree stem. Some say tree skin. It was always dry surrounded by beads all around it. So when rain comes, she will throw it in the air. You will see it flying, instantly it will turn into lightning. Even with the sound with real thunder. And start searching for its victim. I mean to where it's been directed to by the sender.

She showed me all the places where the spirits of the people she killed were living. Some were in a calabash. Hidden in a forest, when it's night time, they will come out and start to patrol. All these spirits are people who died in tragic deaths. I mean their death was premature. So their spirits will be caught by her and used for her own good. Some victims are real humans who died and then after being buried, Witches will call them and come out of their coffins being alive again with their physical bodies. They become slaves to the people who killed them. They even patrol anytime of the day or night but you can't see them, but they see you.

If you go to the grave right now to open your loved ones coffins. You will be shocked, most of them are empty, no signs of corpses.

She said this place I put this thing, that place I put that thing and so on. The next morning Mrs Mayo was coming so she could initiate me into all levels of witchcraft. That night I was going to be initiated, nothing came to sleep with me.

Witchcraft and Voodoo in Africa is almost practised everywhere in many countries surrounding the continents. Whatever the basis of their power and the means by which it is exercised, witches (and sorcerers) are regularly credited with causing all manner of disease and disaster. Sickness, and even death, as well as a host of lesser misfortunes, are routinely laid at their door. Pray is the only weapon to protect you from becoming a victim to witchcraft.

As I was saying I was seeing different kinds of strange stuff and objects mentioning some of it you'll be freaked out right now. If a person who is not a witch sees that, they will die at the spot.

I woke up feeling like I was drunk and tired too much. Around 10 a.m. the next morning Mrs Mayo was already with us and joined us for breakfast. After we started our initiation ceremony. It was a long process and at the end she applied some more witchcraft marks on my body and my shoulders, at the middle of my back, forehead and under my feet. Each of them had meaning. Some were to be strong, some to see more in the spirit realm. Some were for casting spells and some were to make me be able to separate my spirit from my body which is called astral travel or astral projection.

A little bit on that, out-of-body experience, which some might also describe as a dissociative episode, is a sensation of your consciousness leaving your body. These episodes are often reported by people who've had a near-death experience. People, who practice magic, and witchcraft, are often there because for you to operate into the realm of the spirit you have to master this method. Thanks to the initiation marks, it will do the job for us. You have to just lay down with a single chant then wait for the magic to happen.

People typically experience their sense of self inside their physical body. You most likely view the world around you from this vantage point. But during an OBE, you may feel as if you're outside yourself, looking at your body from another perspective

Astral projection is when it comes in place to witches because you can't transfer food from the realm of witches to the realm of the humans to feed them human meat in physical form.

Yes you can go to London or America with or without your body flying. After cutting these marks she applied blood from the chicken, chanting my totem for it to work. We had to burn that chicken until it was finished to finish the ceremony. That was the night I started waking up in the spirit. I remember another fine night; I went with Mrs Mayo, grandmother and Pamela to another house. Grandmother did what she was supposed to do which I can't tell because I will die once I mention it. Within seconds, we were inside the house.

Sometimes witches sprinkle the house and Inside mortuary water for you to sleep like a dead person. The water that was used to bathe the corpse at the mortuary. Once sprinkled this water, you can't move, or wake up. Even if I slap you many times you cannot hear it.

Or they can send a spiritual wind to investigate the house before getting inside. If the wind doesn't come back. She or he will have the right to enter, it means it's safe. But if it comes back, she will run for her life because it's dangerous to enter or stand there. That person is protected either by an angel or charms.

As we entered that house, a woman and her husband were fast asleep, slumbering and naked. We blow his p.....s (sexual organ) with hot air coming from our mouths and become erected by it. Grandmother was the one who started sleeping with that man, followed by Mrs Mayo, Pamela until my turn arrived. It was like we were doing it live, the man was moaning in pleasure in his dream. And we really did enjoy it. Poor to his wife she didn't hear a thing because of the charm we had blown outside the house. We finished and returned back home. When I woke up, I was realising what we did the previous night.

I was now getting used to it and enjoying it as well. We started going to different houses sleeping with different men. That's why many people don't want to leave the witchcraft they enjoy, sleeping with people, eating their flesh. It's like a party every night. You can sleep with anyone you like. Sometimes we were going after their children's meaning in the victim's children to sleep with them and to bewitch them. But most of the time, grandmother was the only one to sleep with men as I was an amateur plus I was still learning.

I was not allowed to sleep with men every day. There are different kinds of witchcraft. I didn't see grandmother going to the graveyards to take human flesh. Maybe she was doing it while she was alone I don't know but Mrs Mayo yes. I went with her several times.

I was given a husband who was an old man, who was killed by my grandmother a long time ago.

When his spirit comes at night, it was my job to entertain the spirit by sleeping with it. Technically, I was its wife. I was shown and taught many things in this realm of witches. Unfortunately, Julia died mysteriously. People heard that her child was bitten by a snake whilst he was sleeping. But it was grandmother and Mrs Mayo's doings, because she was prayerful, she had to go. She was busy working on the field when she was bitten because of that she was chased out of the house to her parents' home. But honestly speaking it was their plan all along. I wrote my final exams and did well not with flying colours but better. But no boy was proposing to me, it wasn't a big deal though because I was having my husband, who was bringing money to me even if I ask for anything.

When I was in form six (Grade 12) that's when trouble started. There was a witch doctor that was hired by people to operate in villages, including ours.

Well; there was this rumour that he lives in a dam. And comes outside when called to do his job, or to perform rituals or being sent. People and traditional healers will go to the river he stays and start doing incantations, invoking him to come out. One of the things they do is to sprinkle rice on top of water. This was to alert the spirits that we are here and in need of help. It was said that he was taken by mermaids and was missing for over thirty years. That's when he became a witch hunter.

His mission was to help people who are bewitched, protect their homes, catch witches and render them useless. Meaning taking their things or killing them if necessary. He was living as well on land, but most of his time would be underwater.

Witches were the ones to quickly spread the rumours that he was in our village already, and was resting at Kings Place. He will start operating tomorrow; everyone must get ready for the big day. We were at school by that time and we also heard the news there. I went home and told my grandmother about the news. She said she heard it already.

Grandmother didn't sleep at home that night. Only came back very early in the morning.

Granny: Amelia I am going somewhere if anybody asks me, tell them that grandmother is gone to a funeral at her rural area, her parents place. If they ask you some questions, do not answer any of them okay. Just say I don't know, wait for grandmother to come. She left us alone again. Around 10 a.m., people arrived. Leading were two king's commanders followed by other three men dressed in animal skins and the rest of the village. This caused fear to pop up instantly after seeing the mob following these people.

Where is your grandmother girls? I want to know why she didn't come to the meeting where there were others. Said one of the commanders.

"She is not here", I answered, stammering and told them exactly what I was told by grandmother to say.

"Let us not waste time, let me start our job," one of the three men said, coming forward. He asked for a plate full of water. Placed it between the yards then dropped a small stick down behind the plate. "Please calm down, I need a strong heart here to prove my powers," he said looking at the crowd, raising his right hand. Even our neighbours were gathering around.

"I want three people with strong hearts, who don't get scared quickly to come forward," he said pointing fingers to where the men were. First men were hesitating but lastly three of them stood to the front. They were told to wash their face and hands in the plate water and to look inside after he dipped his dick. All the men who looked at this plate freaked out. Some jumped out, falling down. They were told to tell what they were seeing. All they responded "snake, a big snake"

Everyone who looked while covering their eyes Sure there was a big snake appearing laying across the plate, twisting and turning. "Wherever your grandmother is, I know she is seeing it in her mirror. When she is back she will witness the destruction I caused to her belongings. She is a very strong witch, a tough one" He wrapped a red cloth around his waist and jumped that stick. He picked it, dropped it down and picked it again. After that I went inside our bedroom. It seems as if that stick was the one dragging him inside. All of us witnessed a hidden power from the stick pulling him towards where it was pointing.

Within minutes he came out running, screaming. Went to the kitchen and did the same thing again. The crowd were singing terrifying songs, killing the witch and rendering them useless.

Another thought of running came but with these men, I won't get far. He then came out running rounding our kitchen as if he was chasing something or being chased. When he was at the back of our kitchen, we had a sickening thud followed by a loud scream once. We heard something falling and all went to check what was transpiring there. He was laying on his back, kicking his legs, rolling his eyeballs and a froth foaming on his mouth.

We all knew that something went wrong. After everyone witnessed this, people ran for their lives in seven ways. They came in one way but we're going in seven ways, showing that it was not a situation to play with. Even the king's commanders, only two of his men were left trying to handle the situation. The sound was like a person hit by a car or a spiritual horn or a lightning. Two of his men took their beloved friend and went back running to try to save his life.

CHAPTER ELEVEN

LET ME MAKE IT QUICK so that I can finalise my story. I know you are already waiting eagerly to hear what happened next. He was taken by his guards after the collision with the spiritual stuff which nearly took his life. Everyone disappeared into thin air after witnessing that terrifying incident. Now the entire crowd was dispersed leaving me and Pamela alone and the witch doctor was taken to the king's

Courtyard to get treated immediately.

We rushed to Mrs Mayo's house only to learn that she was not there also. We hear that she went to her brother's house in another village nearby. I knew that it was her excuse for trying to escape the witch doctor. Three days passed, and people were telling different stories about what happened. Others were saying the witch doctor had died, others were saying he was still receiving treatment at the King's House.

As granddaughters of the witch no one wanted to share with us rumours or to come near us. The fifth-day, the king sent his guards to our house to fetch us. We were brought before the King's Counsel. We went scared to death seriously talking, our hearts we're terrified of what they were going to do next. In my mind, maybe they were going to punish us by the death or the witch doctor to deal with us, or the crowd who were gathered outside to beat us.

It was around six in the morning when we arrived and sat down. One of the guards went inside to report obviously that we were there. He came out with the King. Surprisingly when we arrived all the people were already gathered outside and you can see their eyes were glued on us like vultures waiting for a dying animal to breathe its last breath so that they can feast on it. The counsellor brought the king with his three soldiers and they are not the one who was dressed similar like that witch doctor.

"These are her granddaughters," said the counsellor. They asked our names and we told them. When we are there that's when we told that this is the real witch doctor the man which was wearing similar like the previous one. That one was just an assistant, who had been sent, that one was the real deal. He made us stand, and put a white cloth wrapping snuff inside.

"You Pamela, the light-skinned one, come here first and jump my stick," He said. She jumped for the first time and started screaming and breathing heavily right away. Here comes trouble I said to myself. She was instructed to do it for the second time, but now returning to where she started. The second jump was too vicious; she screamed a louder scream than the first then fell down as if she was dead.

It was such a hair-raising moment; I was scared to do it because I knew exactly that I was next. I don't know what was going to happen to me. The counsellor sitting next to me had a boring attitude and was talkative.

Counsellor: Hey you young witches, this is the real witch killer. That one who has been attacked by your things was just a messenger. He is still learning, and was instructed by this one to go and to do the job whilst he was still finishing with another village as well. He is the one whom you hear living underwater. You have been warned girls.

This man actually caused butterflies in my stomach. I was afraid but he doubled my fear, if not tripled it. Later, Pamela regained consciousness. Her eyes were opened wide rolling every direction; saliva was drooling from her lips.

"Stand up young girl, please lead us to where you hide your witchcraft belongings. Show us the way, said the witch doctor. It left me a little bit confused about when he said where you hide your things. Yes she was a witch but she doesn't have anything. I didn't see her having any, if she was having it she should have told me. Whilst still in dismay, Pamela stood up like a possessed person, with a lot of speed running straight, facing home direction.

Followed by the witch doctor and the rest of the crowd.

We run until we reach home. She went straight and took a pick, then rushed to the backyard and started digging. That day we saw different types of strange things including human body parts, baboons, hidden inside the house. We were living with those things in our house without seeing them. It's only when I was initiated into witchcraft, that's when I started seeing them. But this day was visible to all people. She came inside the bedroom and took granny's clay pots, those three ones including the one of blood. The witch doctor took it and destroyed them without hesitation or fear.

The lightning was included. She went to a nearby tree. Then start digging under it. It was in the eyes of all people, and we're happy of us being exposed.

She buried male sex organs there, three of them and was looking fresh with its arteries showing running blood on them. It was her husband that she was married to spiritually. This amazed so many people including me also. Suddenly, grandmother's goblins started attacking people with stones.

People were just found being stoned with things they are not seeing. They were only seeing stones being thrown. I saw granny's lightning coming out of the smoke.

It was not a good sign; it means it was ready to take off to the skies to form clouds so that it can strike people.

Everyone saw that history wanted to repeat itself. They fled like nobody's business. They just ran and stood at a distance, where they felt it was safe. Only watching from a distance. Pamela was still looking possessed, as I said she was now on her body. Plucking out invisible charms, beads from her body. And threw it onto the ground. When she is unplucking, you will see only her hands in action, but when she throws on the ground, those things will be visible. The witch doctor pointed at her with his stick and she fell down for the second time. This time I thought we lost her because the way she fell was sickening.

"The one who started with this witchcraft here is going to face the consequences' ' said the witch doctor. He placed a rope around Pamela's waist and did what he was supposed to do. After a while Pamela woke up when the witch doctor was about to finish. He instructed people to leave Pamela alone so that she can rest you a little bit. He promised to come back again, and said he tied his snare, that if granny touches witchcraft again she would definitely die.

They were this certain woman who was well known as a prophet. She goes to church every Sunday, not even misses any Sunday. Surprisingly, she was working with demons and was prophesying with a mermaid spirit. Technically she was also a witch. Lots of witchcraft equipment was recovered at her place. And was forced to go into her field and dig out a child she buried. The child was working as a charm for her to have a great harvest every year.

When she dug the child out, the child was alive and still breathing. It has been said that the very same child was being eaten by a crocodile at the river three years ago. You know witchcraft, when the child opens his eyes, he dies instantly. And if you go to that prophet church, when she is healing people, people who fall, crippled people will work. So can we call it the power of God or demons manipulating people? Afterwards, we went to Mrs Mayo's house.

Houses you see, they are more than houses to provide shelter for humanity but witchcraft storage and warehouses of evil.

Mrs Mayo's children refused the witch doctor to operate at her house because she was not there. The owner was not around so it was not the right decision to open people's houses to strangers.

Witch doctor: Okay not a problem at all if she is not around, I just need her photo.

They refused, he asked her for old clothes or anything to do with her, but they refused again. Finally he picked her old shoe which was laying outside and proceeded with his journey. He saw that he cannot win.

We followed him wherever he was going. Indeed this day he got rid of every witchcraft activity in the village. Some were caught with crocodiles, lizards, hyenas, snakes and even buckets full of bees in their house and backyards. Everyone started to believe that witchcraft and voodoo existed. He finished his job at sunrise and went back to the King's House to rest. That's when we started being attacked but what was attacking us was invisible until dawn.

The next day we heard that Mrs Mayo was found dead. The cause of her death was unknown. People only found the body floating on top of the dam naked. It seemed like a person who had drowned to death. This shocked many and left them speechless with unanswered questions regarding her mysterious death of this old woman. We knew that it was the witch doctor's deeds. The next morning he came again to our house to finish what he started and it was my turn.

He said this time it requires our relatives from my father's side for him to help us, it was a difficult task. I was left alone without being helped. Death followed in our village. Mysterious deaths were reported on an almost weekly basis, without knowing the cause.

Grandmother came back after a couple of weeks. She didn't get inside the house, only asked to fetch her favourite bag. I rushed to her bedroom and met her outside. I don't know where she spent the whole day when she came, she slept tomorrow. In the morning she said I should accompany her to that cave where the snake was. Obvious to get back the lost powers but to no avail and I don't know how to explain this. We got lost which was impossible to us. The way to the cave was so well known by us. When we try to figure out the other way, we will accidentally find ourselves in another place near our school. Which was far away from the cave. When we tried to find another way to the cave, we would do the same until we saw it was better to return back home.

The second day she slept again outside. But this time I was the first to try to wake her up. It was strange because the granny I know was always the one to wake us up. When I was walking her up she wasn't responding. Pamela rushed and tried the same until we realised that she was dead.

Death was never a fear of mine until I was this old. The day she died. I never ever wanted to make anyone cry and seeing what death had done to my granny, from this point on I wanted to be immortal. After putting her inside shock caused me to fell down on my knees outside. I crunched through the soil and walked up the room to the house. Throwing my bag down on the antique bed. I peeled off my homeroom sweatshirt, kicked off my nikes and sat down on the bed and I cried.

The worst part of grief is from the second of notification leading up to the funeral. No closure, no celebration, just sadness. Nothing feels right, the next couple of days I would sit in the unshakeable feeling of death.

We hired a cart to carry her body to the mortuary. Only one of her children came to attend her funeral. He is the only one who provided support but other children to help refused.

They had nothing to do with the death of a witch who was killing their children. What happened at a funeral describes itself that indeed it was a funeral of a witch, with few people. She was laid to rest; we remained at his house because I didn't write my final exam. I walked through school with fake smiles and conversations that felt unbearably long. Her death was mysterious, without explanation like other deaths which were happening in the village. People being found dead. Imagine we were small kids.

I thought maybe after she was gone as well her witchcraft. But it was all a lie, I realised that grandmother left us with all the witchcraft stuff to continue the job, and what happened next was horrific.

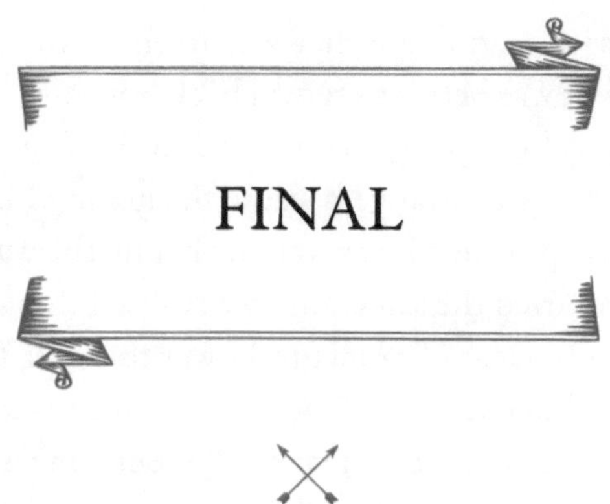

FINAL

AFTER MY GRANDMOTHER'S funeral, her belongings were shared among us. Yes! The granddaughters because of their relatives. Her real children refused to step foot at their mothers funeral. Thanks to the witch doctor, since the day he left I didn't wake up at night to go and witch people at night. Or even to sleep with my spiritual husbands like I was doing before. It seems everything was grinded to a halt but the disadvantage was that there was no income.

First days we tried to resist hunger until we had enough food at our house.

Being hungry is a thing most mature adults can endure for several hours at least. It is uncomfortable, yet adults we try to accept these things and carry on if it is required in caring for the young. The hunger however is a cruelty, a gross and grinding foul cruelty that we must work together upon to defeat it. Such problems should grab our attention and keep it, for a starving and hungry person is a suffering child.

There were lots of livestock before my grandmother died. But after the witch doctor removed everything, they started dying unexplainable one-by-one until none left. You know as people who were adopted to a good life, it was difficult for us to copy this struggling lifestyle.

It didn't end there, the tribulation accelerated to the extent of selling our property clothes, plates and shoes. Only blankets we didn't want to sell and no one was coming to buy. Remember we were witches, no one wanted to get bewitched. The only solution was to start looking for a job. I started at the growth points (shopping centres). One of these shops was vacant. A lady was needed to work as a bartender.

Pamela refused to go and it was my only chance for the job. I worked for two months and left. The money wasn't enough; I left for greener pastures you know in the suburbs along with Pamela.

Finally, I met with a charming, handsome guy called Daniel. I think money was his middle name. He was having everything; it was my first time falling in love with a real person. A great surprise indeed, as you know my story, no man has ever proposed to me, even a mad person. First days I refused to date him, being afraid that anything bad could happen. But pressure was in need of support and he was giving me money after all.

One day he decided to visit me to see my place. I allowed him to do so, to get to know each other. They started chatting with Pamela as I was cooking and they started chatting, bonding with her sister's boyfriend. That's how our relationship with Daniel started. Six months passed with love in the air. It was a free flowing relationship but I was having my secret.

He said I should come to town because he found me a good job at a hardware store. It was because I told him my situation with Pamela that we were orphans struggling with life. Our grandmother passed away due to chronic cancer.

He promised to rent us a cottage so that I can stay with Pamela. How happy and relieved we were. Couple of days he came to fetch us to town just for a walk. We didn't know that the cottage was already waiting for us as promised. I lost count, how many times we thanked him. We started staying and Daniel started buying property bit by bit. Started from plates, stoves and fridge. Television etc. Life started returning to normal and started my job nicely.

Since I started dating with my boyfriend, we never had sex. I was trying to avoid it all along but he started pressuring me for it. One day we were sitting in his car, enjoying life and chatting about what our future was holding. Suddenly we ended up kissing, unintentionally until we ended up having sex. That night Daniel was the happiest guy ever and was in his own world of the everlasting fantasy. After he left in the morning I started feeling dizzy when I was at work. Followed by dry mouth like a person who had run a long race.

I asked to knock off early and they permitted me. When I arrived I laid down on my back on my very bed. Once I fell asleep I saw my grandmother coming to me in a dream. Amelia, who do you leave my things with? You are taking care of yourselves. What about them? I took care of you and this is how you repay me? I took care of you so that you should take care of my things. Now you want to get married how many times?

I woke up to my heart pounding at an incredible speed. Daniel came to see me once heard the news. Suddenly my weight started deteriorating. We visited a doctor and I was diagnosed with malaria.

At first I was lying to myself that maybe my illness was caused by stress and anxiety, or what my late grandmother told me. Visions started popping up every time. Seeing that snake w from the cave. Most of the time it was calling my name, coming out of the cave, charging towards me. When it was about to reach me the vision would disappear. It happens several times until it reaches me then starts licking me or enters my body through my toes.

It turned into reality; Pamela was experiencing the same thing. When this experience takes place, my body will be paralyzed. I spent a couple of days being admitted, doctors were only saying it was malaria. This contributed to the loss of my job. Daniel tried so hard with every fibre of his being to stand with us, providing us food and even paying my hospital bills. Finally, I was feeling better and discharged.

I don't know why it wasn't triggering in my mind that what happened was something trying to send a warning. We started having sex again and our love was on another level. No one has ever seen me that happy. It was my moment and my time.

Until one night after intimacy, as was pulled out his d....k. He held it and screamed like a pain that was in agony. He was pointing his finger down there that something had bitten him.

"Something bit me, look," he said, jumping around the whole house like a kangaroo waiting to fight with its opponent.

I looked at his genitals. What a shocking moment. It was all surrounded by those red big-headed termites, sinking their heads inside his flesh. These things are deadly and not to play with imaging its infestation and damage can be devastating to your home or property, what about human flesh? That's why they are called silent destroyer.

Wherever it bites I was seeing blood gushing out at great heights. Whenever he tried plucking them, it was when they sunk their teeth deeper. This caused someone with a chicken heart like me to run out screaming for help. Neighbours heard the noise, responded quickly in a moment, they were all inside. They asked me what happened, and I felt like answering them. I was still scared also. Daniel was only crying saying, "help, can someone help me, something is biting my p...s"

In such circumstances you can't be shy, shyness will fled. Pamela was not around, there was someone we called Uncle Joe who was also a tenant as well. He was one of the neighbours who came to our rescue. He suggested taking him to a prophet or traditional healers, not a clinic because it was a strange phenomenon. They were only the ones who could help that young man or else he was going to die. He went to call a prophet he knew who was staying close by.

"Do or Die", is what separates one's life to the other. Life is always a do or die situation. Every moment and every second count. It decides our present and our present actions decide our future. Life is not always easy. It is different for each and everyone living in this world.

Everybody struggles with their own hardships and hurdlers These hardships are the defining factors of one's life. They shape a person into what they are. They always come unexpected and leave an unchangeable mark in our lives. Daniel's brother came too, arriving at the same time with Uncle Joe, whom he was back shortly with a prophet. The avenging spirit (the spirit of the dead) confessed to me. It was the spirit that I was given by my grandmother to be my husband. It was totally in rage, breaking windows and furniture, rebuking Daniel to marry me.

"You can't marry my own wife. Sleeping around with her anytime you please. You are going to see me". It said trying to fight Daniel, but people hold me tight.

That moment, I felt like I was dreaming, but aware of my environment. It felt like something was talking inside me but using my voice. I tried standing at the corner after the prophet finished his job. He started removing the termites one by one. This time we're not refusing but it increased the pain. I can tell the type of pain he was in by the way he was screaming, blood started oozing out rapidly.

After he was taken to the hospital to get stitched.

This story surprised many in our country. It was even written in the country's daily newspapers. It's only that we were living in a low-density area so we didn't draw much people's attention or even the neighbours.

Me and Daniel it was over from that day though I tried to persuade him. I was going to get help but he continued saying I was a wife to a dead spirit, a dead person and I wanted to kill him. Remember I am not working now, I lost my job recently. I started doing people's nails. Life went back again to the drawing board. The situation gets tougher and harder, it is unbearable. We went to that prophet, the one we helped Daniel for help. He refused to help us saying our problem was too much for him. In fact, he directed us to another spiritual place where he knows someone who might help us.

But by that time money to go there was scarce as you were not working properly. I tried to borrow money and went to another prophetess nearby to help us. As soon as we stepped foot in her house, we started to be beaten by unknown things including stones. We were able to see whips going up and down touching our bodies recklessly. Even the patients waiting to be helped no one was left to be a victim. The prophet ran to a private room, came out carrying holy water and started circling the whole room sprinkling it. It was a sign of driving away evil spirits then it stopped in seconds showing the power of prayer and God. Every weekend we were going there to remove the witchcraft marks.

What followed after was a long story, the prophet says what was on us was a big problem. She wasn't able to deliver us properly. For the problem to be solved was to me go back to the rural area and something needed to be done there. That is where the root of our problems was or else we were playing with time. We were already initiated into witchcraft; we knew all the tactics and secrets of how to operate in the witchcraft realm. The only luck we had was that we weren't initiated into witchcraft by eating human flesh so there was a huge possibility of becoming an ex witches. Then gave us some spiritual material to use at home.

When we returned back home, I remembered there was no food or even money to go to the rural area. I started looking for a job for about a week. I met with another guy and we only had a phone call. Only talking and video calling.

I was doing this for money not love, I was desperate. Later we met in physical and had sex nothing happened until I was pregnant. Instead of thinking of going to the rural area for our problem to be solved it was all forgotten.

I started spending money on food and luxury things. That's how the devil works right? To make you forget until the damage is done and you are destroyed completely. The time you will come to realise, it will be too late.

My life started changing to normal again. Ummm: it was full of highs and serious lows. I went to stay with my man leaving Pamela but I was sending him money for food and bills. The guy promised to marry me. I will call him Lawrence. He wanted to pay dowry (lobola). I refused him to do that because this money will go straight into my father and stepmother's hands and benefit from that.

Instead, I told Lawrence to buy a new car or to spend it. I delivered my baby boy and two months later he died. We woke him up just like that.

He didn't suck or something, the way grandmother died. Lawrence's relatives started going to the prophets for help. That's when they heard that Lawrence's wife was a witch. They became furious and I was kicked out of the house like a dog.

I returned back to stay with Pamela and started going up and down searching for greener pastures and jobs but things started getting worse. Luckily I had a job opportunity and went there to drop my CVs (curriculum vitae). They called me after working for two months only, someone stole money at the job and they suspected me. I was fired at present for all employees.

When I came back, there was nothing to do or to go. From hero to zero, I became a Barger. Knocking people's houses and in streets asking for money.

There was a house where a lady was needed. I went there and I was employed and I started working. I heard Pamela had fallen sick. She told me that she saw that snake from the cave spitting on her face. All her skin was now peeling off and getting rotten from the inside. I asked for a short leave so I can go and see my sister. In the room she was, smelling her wounds. It was horrible to look at. I took her to the hospital, the money I was having was spent on her medication.

It took a couple of weeks so when I returned back to work they were already employing another maid, meaning it was the end of my job. I started hunting for a part-time job. Every time i slept with a man, I was the one being bitten by unseen things and stopped my menstruation cycle. And ended up beaten severely by them, calling me a witch. Because they were bitten by termites. I can't forget the other day i was beaten so hard that I spent half a month hospitalised

Lastly we decided to go to that spiritual place where we were directed by that prophet. That's when we heard that they moved away from the country and went to Mozambique.

When we returned home, Pamela started to be sick again. It was the stomach ache at first followed by swelling. I decided to go back to the prophet guest house, which helped Daniel for Pamela to be treated. But nothing changed the second day her whole face was swelling with bumps like small horns coming out blood.

I found another job and started working, but an unusual incident happened. Indeed it is a great disadvantage when luck is not on your side. Whenever I get paid that money will disappear from my wallet mysteriously, especially when I planned to take it to a church for the pastor to anoint it.

Now I am the one being bitten by termites. Especially at night when the body relaxed, you can hear them starting digging in my flesh. It closed the doors of one of my incomes which were sleeping with men. There was this lady I worked at her house, she was a successful woman. I realised that she was using charms for her business. She took me to a certain old woman who gave her that charm. She was a powerful herbalist. I was ordered instructions on how to use it.

On our way there I discovered that it was only charms but she initiated people with witchcraft using black magic. It was the same six and nine I returned home. From there it's ups and downs. I tried many prophets, traditional healers, herbalists, nothing is changing. Please help me Pamela is getting worse, I am afraid to lose her. My life is a living hell. Please help me.

Also by Paul Kuipa

Testimony Of The Resurrected
In Love With A Siren
The Walk Of Faith
Amelia The Young Witch

About the Author

Paul Kuipa is one of the best upcoming Aurthors. Born in October in the year 1993, at Dangamvura in Mutare. Which is the second biggest city in Zimbabwe. He grew up in Nyanga in Chinhenga, one of the rural areas. Thats where he finished his primary grade and moved to Harare, the capital city. After his secondary level, he then moved to South Africa, Johannesburg to further his studies. And started his writting career at Unisa College. From there he is unstopped, publishing book after book.

www.ingramcontent.com/pod-product-compliance
Lightning Source LLC
Chambersburg PA
CBHW021755150726
47989CB00004B/1668